SUNSHINE AFTER THE RAIN

SHAQUINA HUNT

DEDICATION

To My Children, I hope you read this and smile. Smile knowing your mother overcame all obstacles. It was each of you that gave me a reason to live.

Shamariyon, Armani, Nevaeh and Addison

ACKNOWLEDGMENTS

Published by: Ideal Book Publishing

Edited by: Trudi Batiste

Graphics by: P2P Branded

Formatting: Abdul Rehman

ISBN:

CONTENTS

FOREWORD
BY: TAMMY JURNETT-LEWIS

Growing up as a little girl, I faced lots of challenges. I was moved around quiet a bit and never stayed anywhere very long. Although I was shuffled from home-to-home, I was always amongst family. In sharing her story, Shaquina Hunts told her journey of her childhood of moving around inside the system of foster care. She also spoke of the abuse projected on to her, as well as her little brother. After being given up for adoption by their biological mother and separated inside the system, the two fought hard to find one another. Although the odds were stacked against them, neither was defeated.

Every year thousands of children are placed in foster care due to circumstances such as being given up by their birth parents, the death of one or both parents, child abuse and other reasons. Every time a child goes in to foster care their chances of normalcy decreases. Many of the children are abused physically, emotionally, mentally and sexually either while in a facility or in a foster home. There are those that find good homes, but the numbers of the ones that don't are greater. Sadly, many of these individuals find themselves either on the streets, in jail or lose their lives to early deaths.

We have to do better as a society to ensure that these children are receiving better care and more support. It is our responsibility as a society to ensure the safety of these children. In Shaquina's story, she shows great courage and bravery. She is the poster child for foster care. She shows us that our past does not define who we are, nor does it have to determine our futures.

CHAPTER ONE:
IN MY FEELINGS

I tried to commit suicide. Seriously. I lost my reason to live. In my mind, everyone was against me...everyone. I was in a dark place and just needed a shoulder to cry on, but there was no one there for me. I knew that I had something to live for, but my heart was empty at the time. Sure, my children meant the world to me, but at that low moment, even my children couldn't save me from the internal battles I faced. Deep hurt and pain consumed me, and I felt misunderstood and lost. I longed to be rescued, but I remained alone with my pain.

It was while drowning in pain that my new profession had become to hurt people and push away those who truly loved me. So, it's no surprise that I was alone. The truth is, I was afraid to open my heart to others because my experience was, anyone who loved me, left me. In fact, the one woman who I trusted to be my protection, my strength, and my shield, left me. I am talking about my mother. I don't think she knew the impact that her leaving would have on my brother and me later in life. Maybe in her mind, it was right to let someone else raise us. I still have many unanswered questions regarding my childhood. For one, why didn't my mother put her pride aside and ask someone for help? Anyone. Why would she just leave us? It was because of her self-ishness and neglect that I have been left with a life-time of disappointment and hurt.

Growing up, I can remember my mother as one of the most beautiful women I had ever seen. Her hair was long, and her skin was as soft as a baby's. Whenever my brother and I spoke of her, we would call her Pocahontas. I try to think of other good memories of her, but only dark and painful memories come to mind. I have this one memory of my brother and I looking out of a window. We saw our mother holding a gun as a group of girls surrounded her. I cried out to her because I thought maybe she had been hurt by them. I don't really remember what happened next. Then, there is another memory of what I remember as "the hand." My brother and I were lying in our bunk-beds and there were what appeared to be a witch standing in the corner of our room. I immediately pulled the covers up over my head and slowly peeped out to be sure my eyes weren't deceiving me. Then, I saw a single hand resting in the center of the floor; there was no arm attached to it. The "witch" tried to pull my brother and I out of bed to step on the hand, but we were too afraid to move. I can't remember if I ever stepped on the hand because when I closed my eyes again, it seemed to be a new day.

This memory is something that I have never been able to forget. Even now, whenever I am in a dark room, I have flashbacks about that hand. I wish I knew the mystery behind it. Although we have never talked about it, I know it couldn't have been a dream because I wasn't the only person to witness these strange events.

On another note, I have often asked myself why evil things happen to innocent children? I mean, why would one sexually assault a three or four-year-old child? It has been difficult to cope with my life after being molested while in my mother's care. While she was enjoying life in the streets, the person whom she trusted to care for me was taking my innocence from me. It makes me wonder if, as a result, there is a curse on my life.

CHAPTER TWO:
REAL LOVE

I can't describe the pain I experienced after real- izing I would never see my mother again. I can distinctly remember the day. She dressed me in a beautiful red and polka dot dress. The sun was shining bright and she sent my brother Dominique and I outside to play. Soon after, she came out and loaded the car with luggage. Once we were all in the car, she drove until we arrived at a church. A little sweet lady came to get us from the car. I could sense something was wrong. My mother kissed my brother and I and then handed our luggage to the little lady. It was in that moment, I knew.

After getting into the lady's car, my brother and I kneeled on the back seat and waved to our mother until she was out of sight. I looked over and saw a single tear roll down Dominique's face. I reached toward him and gently wiped it. Soon after, we ar- rived at another location and was greeted by a beau- tiful family; the Erickson family. Upon meeting them, I was afraid. I did not know them, and I had never seen "white" people before. They seemed to be happy that we were there and made us feel wel- comed. At the time, I was only four years old and Dominique was five. Some of the happiest moments of my life were spent with the Erickson's. Their unconditional love towards us will never be forgotten.

I have so many great memories of my life with the Erickson's. On our very first day of being with them, they taught us how to swim. I was having so much fun that I did not want to leave the pool. My "new parents" were very hands on. I was home-schooled and learned to read and write quickly. My mother, Mrs. Catherine had the best hugs. I would just melt into her arms. My father, Mr. Dennis was just as loving and caring. On Sunday's he would cook us cheese grits which were the house favorite.

The Erickson's were heavily into the church. It wasn't a bad thing. I enjoyed learning bible verses and receiving awards when I quoted scripture correctly. There were church trips and Dominique and I even sang in church. Our parents were good to us and we had many fun and memorable childhood experiences.

As I grew older, I became fearless and enjoyed taking on new challenges. At the same time, Dominique became defiant. He often talked about how much he missed our birth mother. He often became angry and lashed out at others. He began writing letters to better express his feelings. From the letters, I learned that he was afraid of windows and the darkness of the night terrified him. He said he dreamed of wolves with red eyes. As his fears began to consume him, he became more than the Erickson's could handle. Instead of separating us, they thought it best to send us both away.

(Interview with Catherine Erickson)

My son Spence was two months old when I felt a call from God to adopt siblings. It was 5 years later when my husband Dennis agreed to visit New Beginnings Adoption Agency. Although we were looking to adopt older children, we were told that there were only newborns at the agency. We went through their process and received a baby boy in 1994. After one and a half years had passed, we still believed there were siblings who were meant for us. We attended a program by D.F.A.C.S (Division of Family and Child Services) for information on fostering and adoption. We also attended New Beginnings' Annual Adoption Party. There, I shared with a fellow adoptive mom that we were hoping to adopt siblings. Ironically, months later, that same adoptive mom came into the office of New Beginnings as they received a call about placing a brother and sister. She remembered our conversation from the Adoption Party. The director called me on a Tuesday to say that she had siblings for us. We brought them home on Friday, August 16, 1996.

CHAPTER THREE
REGRET

I swear, I should have begged them not to let me go. From that day forward, my life went on a downward spiral. Summer of the year 2000, my life was changed forever. The family who had loved and nurtured me for the past four years stood waving goodbye to us. I didn't understand why we had to leave, but I knew that I needed Dominique and he needed me.

We were transported to another home. The "Matthews" resided in Turkey, North Carolina. As soon as I arrived, I could smell the fresh -cut grass. They lived in a big and beautiful house on many acres of land. The house itself was on a side road secluded from everything else. I was filled with nervousness and excitement about meeting them.

The Matthew's had sixteen kids. Most of them were special needs children with Down's Syndrome and other disabilities. At first, I was fearful because the children were so "different" from which I was accustomed. They didn't talk or act like "normal" kids. When I walked inside the house, there was a big playroom filled with toys. The children were playing with loud toys and the entire scene was chaotic.

As I continued to tour the house, an uneasiness came over me and I knew that I did not want to stay with this family. I longed to be back with the Erickson's, and deep down it pained me to be separated from them.

The first day, Dominique and I remained distant from everyone in the house. The environment was strange compared to any other we had been in before. Mrs. Matthews was an older lady who would mostly sit at the computer all day. Mr. Matthews was very reserved and spent his time building or fixing things in the house. He didn't talk much.

After being there for only a few days, I witnessed things that I had never seen before. When Dominique and I were with the Erickson's, there was no yelling or whippings. This type of behavior was new to us. We were accustomed to being in a peaceful home, unlike this one.

The first few days, Dominique and I could sleep in the same bed, but we were later separated and told to sleep in our own beds. We were then assigned unreasonable chores that were not fit for an eight and nine-year-old. Out of the sixteen children, only five of us were without disabilities. The Matthews made us "normal kids" care for all the other children. We had to feed them, bathe them, and clothe them. Whatever they needed somehow became our responsibility to do. We became like parents, yet we were the ones who were punished when they misbehaved.

Our chores, or as our punishment included having to mow five to six acres of land. We were made to stay outside from sun up to sun down. Can you imagine being kept in 95degree heat and not being allowed to go inside to cool off or to get a drink of water? Out of frustration, we talked about running away even though we knew we would not get far. We were in the country with only dirt roads and woods. We had seen firsthand the severe consequences of being caught. For instance, one of the girls, Christina decided to run away. The family had to look for her and found her in the woods not too far from the house. I can still remember how they beat her and made her do exercises as punishment. We, as kids, were surrounded by hate and became infected by it. So, when Christina was hungry, we made her sandwiches with anything we could find in the refrigerator. It could be peanut butter, cheese, mustard or jelly. Whatever we made, she had to eat it. I wish I could tell her that I was sorry for any part I may have played in her abuse.

Once, Dominique and I were disciplined for not

doing a chore. That day, we were made to sit outside for an entire day. We were not even allowed to go to the bathroom. Our food was brought outside to us and we had to drink from the water hose. We tried to make the best of it by singing and jumping on the trampoline. Reflecting on those memories, I still can't believe how they treated us.

There was another time when all the "normal" kids were chastised and forced to spend the entire winter months in our rooms. All except Megan. She was their favorite. They fed us cheerios for breakfast and peanut butter and an apple for lunch or dinner. As time passed, I became defiant because I was angry and overwhelmed by what I was experiencing. I was tired of walking on eggshells and being isolated from the rest of the world, and I grew tired of constantly being mistreated. The rare times that I was able to eat with the family, I was forced to eat foods that I did not like. I despised Salisbury steak, and everyone knew it. Once, I was made to stand in a corner for hours with my nose against the wall, all because I could not stomach it. I had thrown up at least five times trying to force the meat down. It didn't matter to them. Other times, I would have to sit at the table until I finished my meal. I was so unhappy.

CHAPTER FOUR:
LEARNING TO LOVE

As a young girl, I became promiscuous. I was eleven years old when I was touched by someone inappropriately. I didn't know it was wrong even though it felt so right. It was my thinking as a child. I thought that it was okay for kids to touch other kids. This behavior started a cycle of abuse that I accepted. It made me wonder if a child realized that what they did was wrong, would they be sorry for it? Sometimes, it's hard to tell.

At no time in my life did I ever want to be separated from Dominique. He was my blood brother. He was the only person who never left my side. Unfortunately, there came a time when we had to be separated. It all started when "Kat" put her hands on me in front of my brother. Dominique snapped and beat her nearly to death. The Matthews' plan was to press charges against him, but thankfully it did not happen. Instead, Dominique was removed from the home the following day. When I was finally able to visit him, my eyes filled with tears when I saw him. My brother had grown to be so handsome. Someone made mention that this would be my last time seeing him. I hated that they were right. I never saw my brother again until I was twenty years old.

I had hoped that Dominique was in a safe place now that he was gone. Over time, children's services came out to investigate the incident. I always told the truth about what happened in the home. I wanted out of there, but a week later we moved. It took about seven days to get to our next destination, and I had no idea where we were headed or why. I remember us having to make multiple stops to tend to the special needs' children.

I was twelve years old when we arrived in Tennessee to "the Schmitz" home. They had eighteen children. This family was creepy to me and the house smelled of urine and feces. The home itself was an Old Funeral home in Rutherford. The smell of death permeated within the walls. In one of the rooms, there was a child locked in a cage. More of the children lived in the storm shelter outside.

There was barn out back with horses and other animals. As a way of discipline, another girl and I were made to sit in horse feces all day. We were commanded to choose a pile of feces and to sit in it. I wouldn't wish this experience on my worst enemy.

I was enrolled in school and was picked on because of the way that I looked. My hair was a mess and my clothes were dirty and worn. I wanted to fit in with the others because it was the first time I had been around other black people. When I had the opportunity to speak with a counselor, I shared some of my experiences at the home. Shortly after, we were all removed from the home and placed elsewhere. Eventually, the Schmitz' were sentenced to jail for neglect and abuse. I was happy to testify on behalf of myself and the other abused children in the home. They deserved to be convicted for all the horrible and inhumane things they did to us.

It is hard to love when you are broken inside. To be lost and to have your identity stripped away will cause one to put up a wall against others. In August 2004, at twelve years of age, I was placed with Treva and Kevin. They resided in Dyer, Tennessee, in the country. Treva was an outspoken lady, and she was an avid churchgoer. She was very gifted; she played the piano, directed the choir, and taught Sunday school. Kevin was a military man who did not talk much. They had two children; a son, Dezane and daughter, Jacquetta.

I loved being with Treva. I had never lived with a black family, and I hoped that life would be easier going forward. I fit in with the family from day one. My sister and I had a bond that could not be broken. We were at the age where boys were all we thought about. In the past, I was always isolated from the world. Now that I had the freedom to explore life, I wanted to live life to the fullest.

I became pregnant in the 10th grade. My parents didn't want me to have a child because I was just a child myself. Although, I still had more life ahead of me, I did not want to give my child away. I could not help thinking that I had been given up; I did not want my child to have the life I had.

My experience with pregnancy was beautiful. My baby was going to love me, for me. That simple reality gave me peace on the inside. On August 29th, 2008, I welcomed my baby boy, Shamariyon. I had to learn to take care of him while I was still in school. It was hard at times. Thankfully, my parents were there to step in and help when needed.

Treva showed me how to be a mother. I didn't know how to change a baby properly, or how to fix a bottle. I did not even know how to soothe my baby when he cried; it was all things that had to be learned. I didn't have a job, so I depended on Treva and Kevin to buy diapers and to pay for day care. There were times when they could not afford day-care, so I stayed home from school with my son. There was no one to blame but myself, he was my child and my responsibility. I had to do what I had to do for myself and Shamariyon.

One summer, I stayed with a lady whom I called my aunt. It was a nightmare. Her boyfriend, who was drunk at the time, sexually assaulted me while I was holding my son. I yelled, "You are about to make me drop my son." At that moment, he seemed to come back to reality.

I left the house to find a phone. I called Brushaun. When my mother came home from work, I told her what happened. The guy was arrested the following day. My "aunt" turned her back on me and remained with her boyfriend. When I went to court, my family was on the opposite side of the court-room. I could not believe that they would defend him after what he had done to me. As a result of raping me, he was sentenced to prison for 3-5 years. There were many nights that I was afraid he would send someone to kill me. Surprisingly, after his re-lease from prison, he came to my job to apologize. He completely broke down in tears, and I knew he was truly sorry. I forgave him, and I was finally able to be at peace regarding that situation.

It was the beginning of my Senior year of high school when I found out that I was 6 months preg-nant with my baby girl. I was 17 years old at the time. My stomach was getting rounder, and I was sick a lot, but I didn't want to believe pregnancy was the reason. My child's father was someone of which my mother did not approve. I knew that she would have negative things to say because he was older than I was.

Being pregnant was a big disappointment to my family. In addition, I was trying to graduate high school with now having two children to raise. I was discouraged knowing that I did not have a plan. It wasn't until Mrs. Matthews told me that I was going to be like my mother, that I became motivated to prove her wrong. I was going to succeed, and I knew that determination was going to be the key to my success.

With the help of my parents and a few others, I was able to get my own apartment and graduate from high school with Honors. This was one of my greatest accomplishments. I felt extremely blessed to walk across the stage to receive my diploma.

Times were even harder after graduation. My son and daughter were dependent upon me, so I couldn't just give up. I had a car, but I needed to get a job and secure daycare. I found a job at the Dollar General store, and I registered my children in day care. I was only making minimum wage at the time, so it was stressful trying to make ends meet on a limited income. I began dating a young man who meant the world to me. He accepted me for all my flaws and helped me grow into a mother of which I could be proud.

In 2010, Myspace was still the trend. Dominique

reached out to me, and we reunited after years of being apart. In 2013, I picked him up and moved him in with me. I knew that he had a hard life just as I had. The way we coped with pain was different. We were now young adults, and complete opposites. All that mattered was that he was there with me during the trial and error.

CHAPTER FIVE: REUNITED

Once we were reunited, my brother Dominique came to live with me. It was a challenge. We had grown apart and had to learn and adjust to each other all over again. I was stable; working and living on my own. Dominique had turned into a "street" guy. We often clashed because he did not accept that I liked my home and belongings in a certain way. We loved each other, but there were times we did not get along. You would have thought we hated each other. The demons from our past were still haunting us.

We did have some good days. On those days, we talked a lot about our childhood and how we wished that things had turned out differently. We agreed that we hated our mother and blamed her for the abuse we had suffered. We still carried the memory of her giving us away. Of course, we did not know about all her struggles, and as children, we could only assume.

We agreed that our happiest moments in life were spent with the Erickson family. I cannot begin to articulate the love that I have for them. They were good to us. I tried searching for them on social media, but at the time, had come up empty. I believed in my heart that we would see each other again. I also believed that I would find my birth mother.

One day, I decided to resume my search for my loving family, the Erickson's. I sat down at my computer and typed the name, "Spence Erickson." When I saw the picture, I just knew it was him. The picture was of a young man with orange hair. I started to cry and sent him a message. I was disappointed when I did not get a reply. So, I tried a second time. This time, I typed, "Catherine Erickson." I was so nervous as I sat and stared at a picture of her beautiful face. I was overtaken by my emotions thinking about the impact she once had in my life. I longed to be held by Ms. Catherine because in her arms was my safe place. I sent her a message and surprisingly, she answered. I couldn't believe it, we were speaking for the first time in years. She shared details of the dreams she had of me and how she wondered if we were doing okay. I missed her so much and could not wait to see her again.

Catherine and I planned to meet the following weekend. I was nervous. I was no longer the sweet and innocent child that she once knew. As an adult, I had gotten several tattoos and piercings. I did not want to give her a bad impression or to be judged by my appearance.

Dominique went with me. When we arrived at the house, things were just as I had pictured in my mind. The tree from which we used to jump from as children was still there, and so was the pool where I first learned to swim. I was finally back at home, and it felt amazing. With great anticipation, Dominique and I sat under the porch and waited on our long-lost family to return from church. My stomach was in knots as I saw the car approaching the driveway. The entire experience felt like a dream.

After Dominique and I greeted the family with hugs and tears, we all went into the house. I could smell the aroma of fresh boiled peanuts, and my heart skipped a beat. I was really at home. As we sat and exchanged stories about our lives over the years, I was still overwhelmed by the love this family had for me and my brother. Catherine had kept every picture and video of us. We reminisced about holidays and birthday parties and the pictures told the stories of how happy we were. She showed me a letter from my biological mother which brought me to tears. In it, my mother said she was planning to come back for us, but she never did. It meant a lot to me that Catherine had kept all these memories. She even had the little dress that I wore when she picked me up from my mother. My heart melted inside. For me, this dress signified hope, peace, faith, and purity. The pictures were especially special because I did not have any other memories from my childhood; not even a school project. Thanks to Catherine, I had something of my own to share with my children.

Even after seeing Mrs. Catherine, I was still left with a void. I needed to know if my birth parents were alive and well. Mrs. Catherine did not know much about my birth mother, only what she was told by the adoption agency. She never spoke to my mother directly after we were put up for adoption, nor did she know the backstory. As grateful as I was to the Erickson's for all that they had done for me and Dominique, my search was not over. I had to find my mother.

I remembered that my mother resided in Augusta, Georgia, so I began reaching out to agencies that she may have contacted concerning adoption. A search on Google showed over 1000 stories of children and parents trying to connect with each other. I decided to post a message in one of the forum discussions in hopes that someone would reach out to me. Months passed, and I never received a response. I began to get depressed about it. I had been angry at my mother's selfish actions for so long; I needed closure. I spent days in bed without interacting with my children. I did not want to be bothered by any-one. The days continued to pass with no responses from my search. I felt defeated.

I called Dominique and told him that I was going to post a video on Social media seeking out information to locate our mother. I was desperate. Dominique was hesitant to help, but he knew I was serious. This was something I felt I had to do. Thankfully, I had the support of close friends and others who knew my story and understood my sense of urgency.

CHAPTER SIX:
IN MEMORY OF BRUSHAUN
"PROMISE TARVER"

It was December 7, 2014. My phone rang at 6 o clock in the morning. It was a friend calling to say that my child's father, Brushaun, had passed away. This was hard to believe because I had just talked to him the day before. He told me that he would be picking up our daughter at 8 am which was in just a couple of hours. I knew of a guy with the same name as Brushaun, and maybe, just maybe there was a chance it was the other person. I went back to bed and prayed it was not the Brushaun that I knew.

Once I looked on social media, I saw that it was true. My Brushaun was really gone. As the reality of his passing set in, grief overwhelmed me, and I dropped to my knees and screamed until I could no longer breathe.

I was told that Brushaun and his best friend Joe had left a party and were trailing home behind their cousins. The car they were in was hit head-on by a 16-year-old drunk driver. The car flipped into a ditch, and Joe died on impact. The cousins in the lead car realized that there had been an accident and they jumped out of their vehicle to help.

At the time of the accident, Brushaun was still alive. His cousins tried to pull him out of the car, but he was trapped inside. It was raining which made it difficult to maintain a grip on him. They desperately tried to save him, but they kept slipping into the mud. When sparks flew from the car, Brushaun told them that it was just his time to go. The car caught on fire and by the time the police and fire departments arrived, he had burned alive. His last words were, "what about my kids?" I was heartbroken at the news.

I began to question God. Why would he take this beautiful soul in such a tragic way? Brushaun was a good father who always had my back. We were best friends. Now, he was gone. The drunk driver suffered no injuries from the accident, yet he was responsible for the deaths of Brushaun and Joe. They were great fathers, brothers, and sons. Why God why?

I spent the next year going back and forth to court after the accident. The driver was young and had no remorse for what he had done. Anger consumed me, and I wanted him to die or at least feel our pain. Imagine my devastation when the court ruled in his favor, and he only received probation for his actions. It was so unfair. Because of his negligence, one day I was going to have to tell my daughter that her father burned alive because of him.

CHAPTER SEVEN:
THE MOVE

November 2015, it was time to resume the search for my birth family. I was still recovering from the events surrounding Brushaun's death, and I became more depressed. It had gotten so bad, I didn't want to live anymore.

Since I felt I had nothing to lose, I recorded another video requesting information about my mother and posted it on social media. Within a couple of hours, I received a phone call from my sister's father. My mother had more children after giving up Dominique and me. The man shared with me how much he thought his daughter (my sister) and I looked alike. He also mentioned that he once kept my brother and me when we were children. This was news to me because I did not remember him. He promised to contact my birth mother and give her my telephone number. Thirty minutes had passed when I got the call I had been waiting for my entire life. When I first heard her my mother's voice, she sounded so happy to hear from me. I was just as happy, and all I wanted was to see her and be with her.

Journey to Meet My Family

I didn't really know how to feel. My emotions were all over the place. I was nervous, happy, and then angry. The first stop was North Carolina to pick up my brother so that we would be together on this journey. We were told that the news station was going to be there to film our reunion, so we stopped at the nearest barber shop. When we shared our story with the barber, he gave my brother the haircut for free. Afterwards, we proceeded on our way.

The closer we came to our destination, the less control I had over my emotions. I burst out into tears when I saw the number of family members who stood in the street holding flowers and signs. I couldn't believe there were so many there to welcome us. I was speechless and overwhelmed at the same time. There were screams and loud cries of excitement. We could barely get in the driveway. When we opened the car door, our family rushed towards us making it difficult to get out.

I was happy to finally meet everyone. In the past, I had a few private conversations with family. Some said not to move there because my mother was not being authentic. I chose to move anyway. I wanted to be close to my parents and my siblings. My mother had seven children and my father had two. I was the oldest of my father's children, and he wanted me close to him.

The weekend went by so fast. Honestly, I was ready to get back home. On the ride back, I was happy and reflecting on all that had happened. My sister, (Quetta), seemed sad. She knew, deep down, I wanted to move there. I was her only sister and she wanted me to live near her. I needed to be happy and not just pretend to be happy. I wanted to live my best life...for once. I had made up my mind that this was "my time."

I traveled to Georgia every weekend to try and make up for lost time. After celebrating my sister's birthday and spending Thanksgiving with my mother and the rest of my family, I desired to be closer to them. Being with them filled the voids that my heart had been missing. I felt connected to them, and it was a great feeling.

I decided to step out on faith and move to Georgia to be close to my family. They all encouraged me and said it was a great idea. Although other family members tried to warn me that my mother was not who she portrayed herself to be, it did not change my mind. I even believed some of the things they said, however, I had waited my entire life to be back with my mother. I was not going to pass on the opportunity to build a future with her no matter what the cost,

I discussed my desire to move with my boy-friend, Adrian. As expected, he was a bit skeptical and felt I was moving too fast. In my heart, I knew he was right. After all, I had not worked a job in al-most a year due to complications with my preg-nancy. Money was tight, bills were due, and we had just enough to get by each month. It was a longshot, but my thinking was if we could just get there- it wouldn't be long before we would be on our feet. There was plenty of support; my mother, father, and grandparents were all there to help. I had convinced myself that it was going to work.

I began my search for a place to live. I soon dis-covered that in Georgia, one was required to make 3 times the rent. I had been unemployed for some time, and my credit was not strong enough to work with a realtor, so I took a chance and called my mother to ask if we could move with her. She said yes, but I knew it wouldn't be easy. I had been inde-pendent for so long and moving in with her was tak-ing a step backward in my opinion. The last thing I wanted to be was a burden on her.

My boyfriend Adrian eventually decided that he would take this journey to Georgia with me. I was excited. We had been together for years, and I wanted to spend my life with him. We packed up our belongings and prepared to move.

Having to rent a U-Haul was going to cost us $2000 and we couldn't afford that. We only had about $600 to our name. We called a friend and asked if he would rent us a truck. Because there wasn't a lot of space in the truck, a Dodge Ram, we decided to take only our clothes and leave the remaining things behind. We put our furniture on the side of the road as a "free for all" and headed south.

The ride to Georgia gave me peace of mind. My heart was happy at the thought of having a fresh start. When we arrived, the family was waiting for us. I was so excited. My mother had cleaned out my little sister's room for us. Even though the room was small, we made it work.

The first week at my mother's house was a little hectic. I did not know that my aunt and her kids were staying there as well. Including my immediate family, there were a total of three different families living in one house. At times, it became difficult to have a "normal" day. It was time to put together my plan to regain my independence.

I woke up each morning to write a to-do list. My mother gave me information and told me what I needed and where to go to get things done. First on the list was to find another place to live. I discovered I had a family member who rented houses which was convenient. She showed me a beautiful3 bedroom home in a decent location. Once I walked inside the house, I knew it was for me. I fell in love with it, and it was perfect for my family. I only needed to figure out where I was going to get the money to move in. From that day, I was determined to save as much as could.

My second week in Georgia, I enrolled my children in school. I didn't have a car, and I hated depending on others. That reason alone caused me to rethink moving to Georgia in the first place. I didn't see my mother much. She worked around the clock, day and night. Sometimes, she would come home at 8 am to "check in" before heading right back out.

Old emotions begin to surface, and I began feeling the same neglect I did as a child. I began having flashbacks of the time she left me, and bitterness set in. I felt as if nothing about the situation had changed. It was as if she still didn't have time for me or her four kids after me. I didn't want to seem selfish, but I did not understand how she could give up Dominique and me, then have more kids and treat us as if she did not wrong us all those years ago. It was not long before tensions filled the house, and I knew it was time to go. I could no longer bear to live with her.

Dominique and I both became furious at our mother. In our anger, we went LIVE on social media to answer questions about our lives and to express how we felt about what had happened to us. When my mother found out, she kicked my family and me out of her home. I did not know what we were going to do, but I had to find somewhere for us to lay their heads. I swallowed my pride and went to the family member with the house for rent. I told her the situation and by the grace of God, she worked out a payment plan with me and gave me the keys to the house.

We had no furniture to put in the house, but it was our own place and we were at peace. Most days, we struggled to get our necessities. Adrian and Dominique walked to the store using a baby stroller to transport our groceries. I received help from the state, so being able to buy food was not as big of a concern. I did not want to ask anyone for help. Pride was one of my biggest flaws. Honestly, I felt like they should have offered. I did not understand why the same family who wanted us to move to Georgia did not take the time to make sure we were ok. I felt abandoned, and I could feel my depression creeping up on me again.

The days became longer, and it was getting harder to make our ends meet. Just to have a ride to fill out job application was a challenge. Not to mention, the relationship with my mother wasn't getting any better. I had mixed emotions about our situation; one day I loved her and despised her the next. I had to accept that she really hadn't changed in the twenty years that we were apart.

My financial state was declining fast. I received a check once a month which only covered the rent. Adrian and I had to really hustle up money for the remaining household bills. He did his best. On some days, he planned to go job hunting. Since he did not know the area, he often got lost because he did not know where to get on and off the bus. Still, we had to figure out a way to make this move work for us.

I continued to apply for jobs online. Thankfully, I saw an ad on social media seeking a daycare worker. I applied and was hired immediately. Finally, there would be some additional money coming in. I was grateful to be employed, but the job was not what I had expected. The conditions were poor, and I was not treated with respect. I couldn't quit because there were bills to pay.

It had gotten so bad, I reached out to my mother to vent about it. After speaking with her, I decided to build a little trust with the owners, so they would help me to get a car. I needed reliable transportation to get to work. Although they did help me, the work environment became worse. After a while, I could not continue being abused so I finally quit. The owner did not seem to care which was fine with me because I still had my car.

I found a new job and was able to save some money. Our dilemma was finally getting better. With a car, we were able to drive around and familiarize ourselves with our new city. We still struggled, but each day we were moving forward. Surprisingly, the relationship with my mother also improved. We were alike in many ways, yet different at the same time. Once I was able to share the pain of my past with her, she became easier to talk to. We established a level of trust between us, and I was able to gain the closure that I needed by reconnecting with her.

Each day I am healing from the trauma of my past. I love my mother and I have chosen to forgive her. Because of releasing the deep hurt and pain, we both have grown better. For the first time in my life, when I call on her, she is there for me.

CONCLUSION

My life has not been an easy journey. There have been many ups and downs. Through it all, I followed my heart and allowed God to restore the relationships that had left me broken. Your story may not be mine, but together we can trust God to heal us. I pray that after reading my story, you will be inspired to share your own experiences to help others to heal from childhood trauma.

ABOUT THE AUTHOR

Shaquina Hunt is an entrepreneur, song writer and author. She is a Georgia native and although raised in Dyer, Tennessee has since returned to the State of Georgia. Shaquina is a graduate of Gibson County High School and also attended Bethel College. She has an extended background in customer service and thrives to assist others in overcoming life obstacles by continuously giving them hope. She is the owner of Beautiful Queen Collection. She is also the proud mother of four.

www.beautifulqueencollection.org
www.facebook.com/shaquinahunt
www.instagram.com/shaquinahunt19

55377100R00029

Made in the USA
Columbia, SC
14 April 2019